**A Prayer, Meditation, Examen &
Gratitude Journal in One
to Intentionally Cultivate
Saintly Virtue, Grow in Holiness &
Transform your Life
*Before Bedtime***

"*Prayer* gives us strength for great ideals, for keeping up our faith, charity, purity, generosity; prayer gives us strength to rise up from indifference and guilt, if we have had the misfortune to give in to temptation and weakness. Prayer gives us light by which to see and to judge from God's perspective and from eternity. That is why you must not give up on praying!"

-- St. Pope John Paul II

This Journal belongs to:

_____

My Nightly Examination of Conscience

Date: _____

Opening Prayer:

My Lord and my God,
I firmly believe that you are here;
that you see me,
that you hear me,
I adore you with profound reverence;
I beg your pardon of my sins,

and the grace to make this time
of prayer fruitful.
My Immaculate Mother,
Saint Joseph my father and lord,
my guardian angel,
intercede for me.

I'm Thankful today for...

Thank God for whatever you are blessed and grateful today.

_____
_____
_____
_____
_____
_____
_____
_____
_____
_____
_____

The Best Version of Myself today

Revisit the times and situations in the past 24 hours of your actions.

_____
_____
_____
_____
_____
_____
_____
_____
_____
_____

My Nightly Examination of Conscience

Date: _____

My Sins & Shortcomings today

Revisit the times and situations in the past 24 hours of your actions.

_____

_____

_____

_____

*Ask God for forgiveness for any wrong you have committed
(against Him, yourself and/or another person).*

My Resolution for Tomorrow

Ask God to help you to see what He is asking of you and resolve to do it.

_____

_____

_____

My Prayer Requests

Lift up to God anyone and anything you need to pray for today.

_____

_____

_____

_____

_____

Pray the Our Father.

Closing Prayer:

I thank you, My God, for the good resolutions, affections and inspirations that you have communicated to me In this meditation.

I beg your help for putting them into effect. My Immaculate Mother, Saint Joseph my father and lord, my guardian angel, intercede for me.

My Nightly Examination of Conscience

Date: _____

Opening Prayer:

My Lord and my God,
I firmly believe that you are here;
that you see me,
that you hear me,
I adore you with profound reverence;
I beg your pardon of my sins,

and the grace to make this time
of prayer fruitful.
My Immaculate Mother,
Saint Joseph my father and lord,
my guardian angel,
intercede for me.

I'm Thankful today for...

Thank God for whatever you are blessed and grateful today.

_____

_____

_____

_____

_____

_____

_____

_____

_____

_____

_____

The Best Version of Myself today

Revisit the times and situations in the past 24 hours of your actions.

_____

_____

_____

_____

_____

_____

_____

_____

_____

My Nightly Examination of Conscience

Date: _____

My Sins & Shortcomings today

Revisit the times and situations in the past 24 hours of your actions.

_____

_____

_____

_____

Ask God for forgiveness for any wrong you have committed
(against Him, yourself and/or another person).

My Resolution for Tomorrow

Ask God to help you to see what He is asking of you and resolve to do it.

_____

_____

_____

_____

My Prayer Requests

Lift up to God anyone and anything you need to pray for today.

_____

_____

_____

_____

_____

Pray the Our Father.

Closing Prayer:

I thank you, My God, for the good resolutions, affections and inspirations that you have communicated to me in this meditation.

I beg your help for putting them into effect. My Immaculate Mother, Saint Joseph my father and lord, my guardian angel, intercede for me.

My Nightly Examination of Conscience

Date: _____

Opening Prayer:

My Lord and my God,
I firmly believe that you are here;
that you see me,
that you hear me,
I adore you with profound reverence;
I beg your pardon of my sins,

and the grace to make this time
of prayer fruitful.
My Immaculate Mother,
Saint Joseph my father and lord,
my guardian angel,
intercede for me.

I'm Thankful today for...

Thank God for whatever you are blessed and grateful today.

_____
_____
_____
_____
_____
_____
_____
_____
_____
_____
_____

The Best Version of Myself today

Revisit the times and situations in the past 24 hours of your actions.

_____
_____
_____
_____
_____
_____
_____
_____
_____
_____

My Nightly Examination of Conscience

Date: _____

My Sins & Shortcomings today

Revisit the times and situations in the past 24 hours of your actions.

_____
_____
_____
_____

Ask God for forgiveness for any wrong you have committed
(against Him, yourself and/or another person).

My Resolution for Tomorrow

Ask God to help you to see what He is asking of you and resolve to do it.

_____
_____
_____
_____

My Prayer Requests

Lift up to God anyone and anything you need to pray for today.

_____
_____
_____
_____

Pray the Our Father.

Closing Prayer:

I thank you, My God, for the good resolutions, affections and inspirations that you have communicated to me in this meditation.

I beg your help for putting them into effect. My Immaculate Mother, Saint Joseph my father and lord, my guardian angel, intercede for me.

My Nightly Examination of Conscience

Date: _____

Opening Prayer:

My Lord and my God,
I firmly believe that you are here;
that you see me,
that you hear me,
I adore you with profound reverence;
I beg your pardon of my sins,

and the grace to make this time
of prayer fruitful.
My Immaculate Mother,
Saint Joseph my father and lord,
my guardian angel,
intercede for me.

I'm Thankful today for...

Thank God for whatever you are blessed and grateful today.

_____

_____

_____

_____

_____

_____

_____

_____

_____

_____

_____

The Best Version of Myself today

Revisit the times and situations in the past 24 hours of your actions.

_____

_____

_____

_____

_____

_____

_____

_____

_____

_____

My Nightly Examination of Conscience

Date: _____

My Sins & Shortcomings today

Revisit the times and situations in the past 24 hours of your actions.

_____

_____

_____

_____

*Ask God for forgiveness for any wrong you have committed
(against Him, yourself and/or another person).*

My Resolution for Tomorrow

Ask God to help you to see what He is asking of you and resolve to do it.

_____

_____

_____

_____

My Prayer Requests

Lift up to God anyone and anything you need to pray for today.

_____

_____

_____

_____

_____

Pray the Our Father.

Closing Prayer:

I thank you, My God, for the good resolutions, affections and inspirations that you have communicated to me in this meditation. I beg your help for putting them into effect. My Immaculate Mother, Saint Joseph my father and lord, my guardian angel, intercede for me.

My Nightly Examination of Conscience

Date: _____

Opening Prayer:

My Lord and my God,
I firmly believe that you are here;
that you see me,
that you hear me,
I adore you with profound reverence;
I beg your pardon of my sins,

and the grace to make this time
of prayer fruitful.
My Immaculate Mother,
Saint Joseph my father and lord,
my guardian angel,
intercede for me.

I'm Thankful today for...

Thank God for whatever you are blessed and grateful today.

_____
_____
_____
_____
_____
_____
_____
_____
_____
_____
_____

The Best Version of Myself today

Revisit the times and situations in the past 24 hours of your actions.

_____
_____
_____
_____
_____
_____
_____
_____
_____

My Nightly Examination of Conscience

Date: _____

My Sins & Shortcomings today

Revisit the times and situations in the past 24 hours of your actions.

_____

_____

_____

_____

Ask God for forgiveness for any wrong you have committed
(against Him, yourself and/or another person).

My Resolution for Tomorrow

Ask God to help you to see what He is asking of you and resolve to do it.

_____

_____

_____

_____

My Prayer Requests

Lift up to God anyone and anything you need to pray for today.

_____

_____

_____

_____

_____

Pray the Our Father.

Closing Prayer:

I thank you, My God, for the good resolutions, affections and inspirations that you have communicated to me in this meditation.

I beg your help for putting them into effect. My Immaculate Mother, Saint Joseph my father and lord, my guardian angel, intercede for me.

Date: _____

Opening Prayer:

My Lord and my God,
I firmly believe that you are here;
that you see me,
that you hear me,
I adore you with profound reverence;
I beg your pardon of my sins,
and the grace to make this time
of prayer fruitful.
My Immaculate Mother,
Saint Joseph my father and lord,
my guardian angel,
intercede for me.

I'm Thankful today for...

Thank God for whatever you are blessed and grateful today.

_____
_____
_____
_____
_____
_____
_____
_____
_____
_____
_____

The Best Version of Myself today

Revisit the times and situations in the past 24 hours of your actions.

_____
_____
_____
_____
_____
_____
_____
_____
_____
_____

My Nightly Examination of Conscience

My Nightly Examination of Conscience

Date: _____

My Sins & Shortcomings today

Revisit the times and situations in the past 24 hours of your actions.

_____

_____

_____

_____

Ask God for forgiveness for any wrong you have committed
(against Him, yourself and/or another person).

My Resolution for Tomorrow

Ask God to help you to see what He is asking of you and resolve to do it.

_____

_____

_____

_____

My Prayer Requests

Lift up to God anyone and anything you need to pray for today.

_____

_____

_____

_____

_____

Pray the Our Father.

Closing Prayer:

I thank you, My God, for the good resolutions, affections and inspirations that you have communicated to me in this meditation.

I beg your help for putting them into effect. My Immaculate Mother, Saint Joseph my father and lord, my guardian angel, intercede for me.

My Nightly Examination of Conscience

Date: _____

Opening Prayer:

My Lord and my God,
I firmly believe that you are here;
that you see me,
that you hear me,
I adore you with profound reverence;
I beg your pardon of my sins,

and the grace to make this time
of prayer fruitful.
My Immaculate Mother,
Saint Joseph my father and lord,
my guardian angel,
intercede for me.

I'm Thankful today for...

Thank God for whatever you are blessed and grateful today.

_____
_____
_____
_____
_____
_____
_____
_____
_____
_____
_____
_____

The Best Version of Myself today

Revisit the times and situations in the past 24 hours of your actions.

_____
_____
_____
_____
_____
_____
_____
_____
_____
_____

My Nightly Examination of Conscience

Date: _____

My Sins & Shortcomings today

Revisit the times and situations in the past 24 hours of your actions.

_____

_____

_____

_____

Ask God for forgiveness for any wrong you have committed
(against Him, yourself and/or another person).

My Resolution for Tomorrow

Ask God to help you to see what He is asking of you and resolve to do it.

_____

_____

_____

_____

My Prayer Requests

Lift up to God anyone and anything you need to pray for today.

_____

_____

_____

_____

_____

Pray the Our Father.

Closing Prayer:

I thank you, My God,
for the good resolutions,
affections and inspirations
that you have
communicated to me
in this meditation.

I beg your help for
putting them into effect.
My Immaculate Mother,
Saint Joseph my father and lord,
my guardian angel,
intercede for me.

My Nightly Examination of Conscience

Date: _____

Opening Prayer:

My Lord and my God,
I firmly believe that you are here;
that you see me,
that you hear me,
I adore you with profound reverence;
I beg your pardon of my sins,

and the grace to make this time
of prayer fruitful.
My Immaculate Mother,
Saint Joseph my father and lord,
my guardian angel,
intercede for me.

I'm Thankful today for...

Thank God for whatever you are blessed and grateful today.

_____
_____
_____
_____
_____
_____
_____
_____
_____
_____
_____
_____

The Best Version of Myself today

Revisit the times and situations in the past 24 hours of your actions.

_____
_____
_____
_____
_____
_____
_____
_____
_____
_____

My Nightly Examination of Conscience

Date: _____

My Sins & Shortcomings today

Revisit the times and situations in the past 24 hours of your actions.

_____
_____
_____
_____

Ask God for forgiveness for any wrong you have committed
(against Him, yourself and/or another person).

My Resolution for Tomorrow

Ask God to help you to see what He is asking of you and resolve to do it.

_____
_____
_____
_____

My Prayer Requests

Lift up to God anyone and anything you need to pray for today.

_____
_____
_____
_____
_____

Pray the Our Father.

Closing Prayer:

I thank you, My God, for the good resolutions, affections and inspirations that you have communicated to me in this meditation.

I beg your help for putting them into effect. My Immaculate Mother, Saint Joseph my father and lord, my guardian angel, intercede for me.

My Nightly Examination of Conscience

Date: _____

Opening Prayer:

My Lord and my God,
I firmly believe that you are here;
that you see me,
that you hear me,
I adore you with profound reverence;
I beg your pardon of my sins,

and the grace to make this time
of prayer fruitful.
My Immaculate Mother,
Saint Joseph my father and lord,
my guardian angel,
intercede for me.

I'm Thankful today for...

Thank God for whatever you are blessed and grateful today.

_____

_____

_____

_____

_____

_____

_____

_____

_____

_____

_____

The Best Version of Myself today

Revisit the times and situations in the past 24 hours of your actions.

_____

_____

_____

_____

_____

_____

_____

_____

_____

_____

My Nightly Examination of Conscience

Date: _____

My Sins & Shortcomings today

Revisit the times and situations in the past 24 hours of your actions.

_____
_____
_____
_____

Ask God for forgiveness for any wrong you have committed
(against Him, yourself and/or another person).

My Resolution for Tomorrow

Ask God to help you to see what He is asking of you and resolve to do it.

_____
_____
_____
_____

My Prayer Requests

Lift up to God anyone and anything you need to pray for today.

_____
_____
_____
_____
_____

Pray the Our Father.

Closing Prayer:

I thank you, My God, for the good resolutions, affections and inspirations that you have communicated to me in this meditation. I beg your help for putting them into effect. My Immaculate Mother, Saint Joseph my father and lord, my guardian angel, intercede for me.

My Nightly Examination of Conscience

Date: _____

Opening Prayer:

My Lord and my God,
I firmly believe that you are here;
that you see me,
that you hear me,
I adore you with profound reverence;
I beg your pardon of my sins,

and the grace to make this time
of prayer fruitful.
My Immaculate Mother,
Saint Joseph my father and lord,
my guardian angel,
intercede for me.

I'm Thankful today for...

Thank God for whatever you are blessed and grateful today.

_____
_____
_____
_____
_____
_____
_____
_____
_____
_____
_____

The Best Version of Myself today

Revisit the times and situations in the past 24 hours of your actions.

_____
_____
_____
_____
_____
_____
_____
_____
_____
_____

My Nightly Examination of Conscience

Date: _____

My Sins & Shortcomings today

Revisit the times and situations in the past 24 hours of your actions.

_____
_____
_____
_____

Ask God for forgiveness for any wrong you have committed
(against Him, yourself and/or another person).

My Resolution for Tomorrow

Ask God to help you to see what He is asking of you and resolve to do it.

_____
_____
_____
_____

My Prayer Requests

Lift up to God anyone and anything you need to pray for today.

_____
_____
_____
_____
_____

Pray the Our Father.

Closing Prayer:

I thank you, My God, for the good resolutions, affections and inspirations that you have communicated to me in this meditation.

I beg your help for putting them into effect. My Immaculate Mother, Saint Joseph my father and lord, my guardian angel, intercede for me.

My Nightly Examination of Conscience

Date: _____

Opening Prayer:

My Lord and my God,
I firmly believe that you are here;
that you see me,
that you hear me,
I adore you with profound reverence;
I beg your pardon of my sins,

and the grace to make this time
of prayer fruitful.
My Immaculate Mother,
Saint Joseph my father and lord,
my guardian angel,
intercede for me.

I'm Thankful today for...

Thank God for whatever you are blessed and grateful today.

_____
_____
_____
_____
_____
_____
_____
_____
_____
_____
_____

The Best Version of Myself today

Revisit the times and situations in the past 24 hours of your actions.

_____
_____
_____
_____
_____
_____
_____
_____
_____
_____

My Nightly Examination of Conscience

Date: _____

My Sins & Shortcomings today

Revisit the times and situations in the past 24 hours of your actions.

_____

_____

_____

_____

Ask God for forgiveness for any wrong you have committed
(against Him, yourself and/or another person).

My Resolution for Tomorrow

Ask God to help you to see what He is asking of you and resolve to do it.

_____

_____

_____

_____

My Prayer Requests

Lift up to God anyone and anything you need to pray for today.

_____

_____

_____

_____

_____

Pray the Our Father.

Closing Prayer:

I thank you, My God, for the good resolutions, affections and inspirations that you have communicated to me in this meditation.

I beg your help for putting them into effect. My Immaculate Mother, Saint Joseph my father and lord, my guardian angel, intercede for me.

My Nightly Examination of Conscience

Date: _____

Opening Prayer:

My Lord and my God,
I firmly believe that you are here;
that you see me,
that you hear me,
I adore you with profound reverence;
I beg your pardon of my sins,
and the grace to make this time
of prayer fruitful.
My Immaculate Mother,
Saint Joseph my father and lord,
my guardian angel,
intercede for me.

I'm Thankful today for...

Thank God for whatever you are blessed and grateful today.

_____

_____

_____

_____

_____

_____

_____

_____

_____

_____

_____

The Best Version of Myself today

Revisit the times and situations in the past 24 hours of your actions.

_____

_____

_____

_____

_____

_____

_____

_____

_____

_____

My Nightly Examination of Conscience

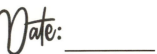

Date: _____

My Sins & Shortcomings today

Revisit the times and situations in the past 24 hours of your actions.

_____

_____

_____

_____

Ask God for forgiveness for any wrong you have committed
(against Him, yourself and/or another person).

My Resolution for Tomorrow

Ask God to help you to see what He is asking of you and resolve to do it.

_____

_____

_____

_____

My Prayer Requests

Lift up to God anyone and anything you need to pray for today.

_____

_____

_____

_____

_____

Pray the Our Father.

Closing Prayer:

I thank you, My God, for the good resolutions, affections and inspirations that you have communicated to me in this meditation.

I beg your help for putting them into effect. My Immaculate Mother, Saint Joseph my father and lord, my guardian angel, intercede for me.

My Nightly Examination of Conscience

Date: _____

Opening Prayer:

My Lord and my God,
I firmly believe that you are here;
that you see me,
that you hear me,
I adore you with profound reverence;
I beg your pardon of my sins,

and the grace to make this time
of prayer fruitful.
My Immaculate Mother,
Saint Joseph my father and lord,
my guardian angel,
intercede for me.

I'm Thankful today for...

Thank God for whatever you are blessed and grateful today.

_____
_____
_____
_____
_____
_____
_____
_____
_____
_____
_____

The Best Version of Myself today

Revisit the times and situations in the past 24 hours of your actions.

_____
_____
_____
_____
_____
_____
_____
_____
_____

My Nightly Examination of Conscience

Date: _____

My Sins & Shortcomings today

Revisit the times and situations in the past 24 hours of your actions.

_____
_____
_____
_____

Ask God for forgiveness for any wrong you have committed
(against Him, yourself and/or another person).

My Resolution for Tomorrow

Ask God to help you to see what He is asking of you and resolve to do it.

_____
_____
_____
_____

My Prayer Requests

Lift up to God anyone and anything you need to pray for today.

_____
_____
_____
_____
_____

Pray the Our Father.

Closing Prayer:

I thank you, My God, for the good resolutions, affections and inspirations that you have communicated to me In this meditation.

I beg your help for putting them into effect. My Immaculate Mother, Saint Joseph my father and lord, my guardian angel, intercede for me.

My Nightly Examination of Conscience

Date: _____

Opening Prayer:

My Lord and my God,
I firmly believe that you are here;
that you see me,
that you hear me,
I adore you with profound reverence;
I beg your pardon of my sins,
and the grace to make this time
of prayer fruitful.
My Immaculate Mother,
Saint Joseph my father and lord,
my guardian angel,
intercede for me.

I'm Thankful today for...

Thank God for whatever you are blessed and grateful today.

_____
_____
_____
_____
_____
_____
_____
_____
_____
_____

The Best Version of Myself today

Revisit the times and situations in the past 24 hours of your actions.

_____
_____
_____
_____
_____
_____
_____
_____
_____

My Nightly Examination of Conscience

Date: _____

My Sins & Shortcomings today

Revisit the times and situations in the past 24 hours of your actions.

_____
_____
_____
_____

Ask God for forgiveness for any wrong you have committed
(against Him, yourself and/or another person).

My Resolution for Tomorrow

Ask God to help you to see what He is asking of you and resolve to do it.

_____
_____
_____
_____

My Prayer Requests

Lift up to God anyone and anything you need to pray for today.

_____
_____
_____
_____
_____

Pray the Our Father.

Closing Prayer:

I thank you, My God, for the good resolutions, affections and inspirations that you have communicated to me in this meditation.

I beg your help for putting them into effect. My Immaculate Mother, Saint Joseph my father and lord, my guardian angel, intercede for me.

My Nightly Examination of Conscience

Date: _____

Opening Prayer:

My Lord and my God,
I firmly believe that you are here;
that you see me,
that you hear me,
I adore you with profound reverence;
I beg your pardon of my sins,
and the grace to make this time
of prayer fruitful.
My Immaculate Mother,
Saint Joseph my father and lord,
my guardian angel,
intercede for me.

I'm Thankful today for...

Thank God for whatever you are blessed and grateful today.

_____
_____
_____
_____
_____
_____
_____
_____
_____
_____
_____
_____

The Best Version of Myself today

Revisit the times and situations in the past 24 hours of your actions.

_____
_____
_____
_____
_____
_____
_____
_____
_____
_____

My Nightly Examination of Conscience

Date: _____

My Sins & Shortcomings today

Revisit the times and situations in the past 24 hours of your actions.

_____

_____

_____

_____

*Ask God for forgiveness for any wrong you have committed
(against Him, yourself and/or another person).*

My Resolution for Tomorrow

Ask God to help you to see what He is asking of you and resolve to do it.

_____

_____

_____

_____

My Prayer Requests

Lift up to God anyone and anything you need to pray for today.

_____

_____

_____

_____

_____

Pray the Our Father.

Closing Prayer:

*I thank you, My God,
for the good resolutions,
affections and inspirations
that you have
communicated to me
in this meditation.*

*I beg your help for
putting them into effect.
My Immaculate Mother,
Saint Joseph my father and lord,
my guardian angel,
intercede for me.*

My Nightly Examination of Conscience

Date: _____

Opening Prayer:

My Lord and my God,
I firmly believe that you are here;
that you see me,
that you hear me,
I adore you with profound reverence;
I beg your pardon of my sins,
and the grace to make this time
of prayer fruitful.
My Immaculate Mother,
Saint Joseph my father and lord,
my guardian angel,
intercede for me.

I'm Thankful today for...

Thank God for whatever you are blessed and grateful today.

_____

_____

_____

_____

_____

_____

_____

_____

_____

_____

_____

The Best Version of Myself today

Revisit the times and situations in the past 24 hours of your actions.

_____

_____

_____

_____

_____

_____

_____

_____

_____

My Nightly Examination of Conscience

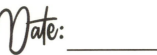

Date: _____

My Sins & Shortcomings today

Revisit the times and situations in the past 24 hours of your actions.

_____

_____

_____

_____

Ask God for forgiveness for any wrong you have committed
(against Him, yourself and/or another person).

My Resolution for Tomorrow

Ask God to help you to see what He is asking of you and resolve to do it.

_____

_____

_____

_____

My Prayer Requests

Lift up to God anyone and anything you need to pray for today.

_____

_____

_____

_____

_____

Pray the Our Father.

Closing Prayer:

I thank you, My God, for the good resolutions, affections and inspirations that you have communicated to me in this meditation.

I beg your help for putting them into effect. My Immaculate Mother, Saint Joseph my father and lord, my guardian angel, intercede for me.

My Nightly Examination of Conscience

Date: _____

Opening Prayer:

My Lord and my God,
I firmly believe that you are here;
that you see me,
that you hear me,
I adore you with profound reverence;
I beg your pardon of my sins,

and the grace to make this time
of prayer fruitful.
My Immaculate Mother,
Saint Joseph my father and lord,
my guardian angel,
intercede for me.

I'm Thankful today for...

Thank God for whatever you are blessed and grateful today.

_____
_____
_____
_____
_____
_____
_____
_____
_____
_____
_____

The Best Version of Myself today

Revisit the times and situations in the past 24 hours of your actions.

_____
_____
_____
_____
_____
_____
_____
_____
_____

My Nightly Examination of Conscience

Date: _____

My Sins & Shortcomings today

Revisit the times and situations in the past 24 hours of your actions.

_____

_____

_____

_____

*Ask God for forgiveness for any wrong you have committed
(against Him, yourself and/or another person).*

My Resolution for Tomorrow

Ask God to help you to see what He is asking of you and resolve to do it.

_____

_____

_____

_____

My Prayer Requests

Lift up to God anyone and anything you need to pray for today.

_____

_____

_____

_____

_____

Pray the Our Father.

Closing Prayer:

I thank you, My God, for the good resolutions, affections and inspirations that you have communicated to me in this meditation.

I beg your help for putting them into effect. My Immaculate Mother, Saint Joseph my father and lord, my guardian angel, intercede for me.

My Nightly Examination of Conscience

Date: _____

Opening Prayer:

My Lord and my God,
I firmly believe that you are here;
that you see me,
that you hear me,
I adore you with profound reverence;
I beg your pardon of my sins,
and the grace to make this time
of prayer fruitful.
My Immaculate Mother,
Saint Joseph my father and lord,
my guardian angel,
intercede for me.

I'm Thankful today for...

Thank God for whatever you are blessed and grateful today.

_____
_____
_____
_____
_____
_____
_____
_____
_____
_____
_____

The Best Version of Myself today

Revisit the times and situations in the past 24 hours of your actions.

_____
_____
_____
_____
_____
_____
_____
_____
_____
_____

My Nightly Examination of Conscience

Date: _____

My Sins & Shortcomings today

Revisit the times and situations in the past 24 hours of your actions.

_____

_____

_____

_____

Ask God for forgiveness for any wrong you have committed
(against Him, yourself and/or another person).

My Resolution for Tomorrow

Ask God to help you to see what He is asking of you and resolve to do it.

_____

_____

_____

_____

My Prayer Requests

Lift up to God anyone and anything you need to pray for today.

_____

_____

_____

_____

_____

Pray the Our Father.

Closing Prayer:

I thank you, My God, for the good resolutions, affections and inspirations that you have communicated to me in this meditation.

I beg your help for putting them into effect. My Immaculate Mother, Saint Joseph my father and lord, my guardian angel, intercede for me.

Date: _____

My Nightly Examination of Conscience

Opening Prayer:

My Lord and my God,
I firmly believe that you are here;
that you see me,
that you hear me,
I adore you with profound reverence;
I beg your pardon of my sins,

and the grace to make this time
of prayer fruitful.
My Immaculate Mother,
Saint Joseph my father and lord,
my guardian angel,
intercede for me.

I'm Thankful today for...

Thank God for whatever you are blessed and grateful today.

_____

_____

_____

_____

_____

_____

_____

_____

_____

_____

The Best Version of Myself today

Revisit the times and situations in the past 24 hours of your actions.

_____

_____

_____

_____

_____

_____

_____

_____

_____

My Nightly Examination of Conscience

Date: _____

My Sins & Shortcomings today

Revisit the times and situations in the past 24 hours of your actions.

_____

_____

_____

_____

*Ask God for forgiveness for any wrong you have committed
(against Him, yourself and/or another person).*

My Resolution for Tomorrow

Ask God to help you to see what He is asking of you and resolve to do it.

_____

_____

_____

_____

My Prayer Requests

Lift up to God anyone and anything you need to pray for today.

_____

_____

_____

_____

_____

Pray the Our Father.

Closing Prayer:

I thank you, My God, for the good resolutions, affections and inspirations that you have communicated to me in this meditation.

I beg your help for putting them into effect. My Immaculate Mother, Saint Joseph my father and lord, my guardian angel, intercede for me.

Date: _____

Opening Prayer:

My Lord and my God,
I firmly believe that you are here;
that you see me,
that you hear me,
I adore you with profound reverence;
I beg your pardon of my sins,

and the grace to make this time
of prayer fruitful.
My Immaculate Mother,
Saint Joseph my father and lord,
my guardian angel,
intercede for me.

I'm Thankful today for...

Thank God for whatever you are blessed and grateful today.

_____

_____

_____

_____

_____

_____

_____

_____

_____

_____

_____

The Best Version of Myself today

Revisit the times and situations in the past 24 hours of your actions.

_____

_____

_____

_____

_____

_____

_____

_____

_____

My Nightly Examination of Conscience

Date: _____

My Sins & Shortcomings today

Revisit the times and situations in the past 24 hours of your actions.

_____

_____

_____

_____

*Ask God for forgiveness for any wrong you have committed
(against Him, yourself and/or another person).*

My Resolution for Tomorrow

Ask God to help you to see what He is asking of you and resolve to do it.

_____

_____

_____

_____

My Prayer Requests

Lift up to God anyone and anything you need to pray for today.

_____

_____

_____

_____

_____

Pray the Our Father.

Closing Prayer:

*I thank you, My God,
for the good resolutions,
affections and inspirations
that you have
communicated to me
in this meditation.*

*I beg your help for
putting them into effect.
My Immaculate Mother,
Saint Joseph my father and lord,
my guardian angel,
intercede for me.*

My Nightly Examination of Conscience

Date: _____

Opening Prayer:

My Lord and my God,
I firmly believe that you are here;
that you see me,
that you hear me,
I adore you with profound reverence;
I beg your pardon of my sins,
and the grace to make this time
of prayer fruitful.
My Immaculate Mother,
Saint Joseph my father and lord,
my guardian angel,
intercede for me.

I'm Thankful today for...

Thank God for whatever you are blessed and grateful today.

_____

_____

_____

_____

_____

_____

_____

_____

_____

_____

_____

The Best Version of Myself today

Revisit the times and situations in the past 24 hours of your actions.

_____

_____

_____

_____

_____

_____

_____

_____

_____

_____

My Nightly Examination of Conscience

Date: _____

My Sins & Shortcomings today

Revisit the times and situations in the past 24 hours of your actions.

_____
_____
_____
_____

Ask God for forgiveness for any wrong you have committed
(against Him, yourself and/or another person).

My Resolution for Tomorrow

Ask God to help you to see what He is asking of you and resolve to do it.

_____
_____
_____
_____

My Prayer Requests

Lift up to God anyone and anything you need to pray for today.

_____
_____
_____
_____
_____

Pray the Our Father.

Closing Prayer:

I thank you, My God, for the good resolutions, affections and inspirations that you have communicated to me in this meditation.

I beg your help for putting them into effect. My Immaculate Mother, Saint Joseph my father and lord, my guardian angel, intercede for me.

My Nightly Examination of Conscience

Date: _____

Opening Prayer:

My Lord and my God,
I firmly believe that you are here;
that you see me,
that you hear me,
I adore you with profound reverence;
I beg your pardon of my sins,

and the grace to make this time
of prayer fruitful.
My Immaculate Mother,
Saint Joseph my father and lord,
my guardian angel,
intercede for me.

I'm Thankful today for...

Thank God for whatever you are blessed and grateful today.

_____
_____
_____
_____
_____
_____
_____
_____
_____
_____
_____
_____

The Best Version of Myself today

Revisit the times and situations in the past 24 hours of your actions.

_____
_____
_____
_____
_____
_____
_____
_____
_____
_____

My Nightly Examination of Conscience

Date: _____

My Sins & Shortcomings today

Revisit the times and situations in the past 24 hours of your actions.

_____

_____

_____

_____

Ask God for forgiveness for any wrong you have committed
(against Him, yourself and/or another person).

My Resolution for Tomorrow

Ask God to help you to see what He is asking of you and resolve to do it.

_____

_____

_____

_____

My Prayer Requests

Lift up to God anyone and anything you need to pray for today.

_____

_____

_____

_____

_____

Pray the Our Father.

Closing Prayer:

I thank you, My God, for the good resolutions, affections and inspirations that you have communicated to me In this meditation.

I beg your help for putting them into effect. My Immaculate Mother, Saint Joseph my father and lord, my guardian angel, intercede for me.

My Nightly Examination of Conscience

Date: _____

Opening Prayer:

My Lord and my God,
I firmly believe that you are here;
that you see me,
that you hear me,
I adore you with profound reverence;
I beg your pardon of my sins,

and the grace to make this time
of prayer fruitful.
My Immaculate Mother,
Saint Joseph my father and lord,
my guardian angel,
intercede for me.

I'm Thankful today for...

Thank God for whatever you are blessed and grateful today.

_____

_____

_____

_____

_____

_____

_____

_____

_____

_____

_____

The Best Version of Myself today

Revisit the times and situations in the past 24 hours of your actions.

_____

_____

_____

_____

_____

_____

_____

_____

_____

My Nightly Examination of Conscience

Date: _____

My Sins & Shortcomings today

Revisit the times and situations in the past 24 hours of your actions.

_____

_____

_____

_____

Ask God for forgiveness for any wrong you have committed
(against Him, yourself and/or another person).

My Resolution for Tomorrow

Ask God to help you to see what He is asking of you and resolve to do it.

_____

_____

_____

_____

My Prayer Requests

Lift up to God anyone and anything you need to pray for today.

_____

_____

_____

_____

_____

Pray the Our Father.

Closing Prayer:

I thank you, My God,
for the good resolutions,
affections and inspirations
that you have
communicated to me
in this meditation.

I beg your help for
putting them into effect.
My Immaculate Mother,
Saint Joseph my father and lord,
my guardian angel,
intercede for me.

My Nightly Examination of Conscience

Date: _____

Opening Prayer:

My Lord and my God,
I firmly believe that you are here;
that you see me,
that you hear me,
I adore you with profound reverence;
I beg your pardon of my sins,

and the grace to make this time
of prayer fruitful.
My Immaculate Mother,
Saint Joseph my father and lord,
my guardian angel,
intercede for me.

I'm Thankful today for...

Thank God for whatever you are blessed and grateful today.

_____

_____

_____

_____

_____

_____

_____

_____

_____

_____

_____

The Best Version of Myself today

Revisit the times and situations in the past 24 hours of your actions.

_____

_____

_____

_____

_____

_____

_____

_____

_____

_____

My Nightly Examination of Conscience

Date: _____

My Sins & Shortcomings today

Revisit the times and situations in the past 24 hours of your actions.

_____

_____

_____

_____

*Ask God for forgiveness for any wrong you have committed
(against Him, yourself and/or another person).*

My Resolution for Tomorrow

Ask God to help you to see what He is asking of you and resolve to do it.

_____

_____

_____

_____

My Prayer Requests

Lift up to God anyone and anything you need to pray for today.

_____

_____

_____

_____

_____

Pray the Our Father.

Closing Prayer:

I thank you, My God, for the good resolutions, affections and inspirations that you have communicated to me in this meditation. I beg your help for putting them into effect. My Immaculate Mother, Saint Joseph my father and lord, my guardian angel, intercede for me.

My Nightly Examination of Conscience

Date: _____

Opening Prayer:

My Lord and my God,
I firmly believe that you are here;
that you see me,
that you hear me,
I adore you with profound reverence;
I beg your pardon of my sins,

and the grace to make this time
of prayer fruitful.
My Immaculate Mother,
Saint Joseph my father and lord,
my guardian angel,
intercede for me.

I'm Thankful today for...

Thank God for whatever you are blessed and grateful today.

_____

_____

_____

_____

_____

_____

_____

_____

_____

_____

_____

The Best Version of Myself today

Revisit the times and situations in the past 24 hours of your actions.

_____

_____

_____

_____

_____

_____

_____

_____

_____

_____

My Nightly Examination of Conscience

Date: _____

My Sins & Shortcomings today

Revisit the times and situations in the past 24 hours of your actions.

_____
_____
_____
_____

Ask God for forgiveness for any wrong you have committed
(against Him, yourself and/or another person).

My Resolution for Tomorrow

Ask God to help you to see what He is asking of you and resolve to do it.

_____
_____
_____
_____

My Prayer Requests

Lift up to God anyone and anything you need to pray for today.

_____
_____
_____
_____
_____

Pray the Our Father.

Closing Prayer:

I thank you, My God, for the good resolutions, affections and inspirations that you have communicated to me in this meditation. I beg your help for putting them into effect. My Immaculate Mother, Saint Joseph my father and lord, my guardian angel, intercede for me.

My Nightly Examination of Conscience

Date: _____

Opening Prayer:

My Lord and my God,
I firmly believe that you are here;
that you see me,
that you hear me,
I adore you with profound reverence;
I beg your pardon of my sins,

and the grace to make this time
of prayer fruitful.
My Immaculate Mother,
Saint Joseph my father and lord,
my guardian angel,
intercede for me.

I'm Thankful today for...

Thank God for whatever you are blessed and grateful today.

_____
_____
_____
_____
_____
_____
_____
_____
_____
_____
_____
_____

The Best Version of Myself today

Revisit the times and situations in the past 24 hours of your actions.

_____
_____
_____
_____
_____
_____
_____
_____
_____
_____
_____

Date: _____

My Sins & Shortcomings today

Revisit the times and situations in the past 24 hours of your actions.

_____
_____
_____
_____

Ask God for forgiveness for any wrong you have committed
(against Him, yourself and/or another person).

My Resolution for Tomorrow

Ask God to help you to see what He is asking of you and resolve to do it.

_____
_____
_____
_____

My Prayer Requests

Lift up to God anyone and anything you need to pray for today.

_____
_____
_____
_____
_____

Pray the Our Father.

Closing Prayer:

I thank you, My God, for the good resolutions, affections and inspirations that you have communicated to me In this meditation.

I beg your help for putting them into effect. My Immaculate Mother, Saint Joseph my father and lord, my guardian angel, intercede for me.

My Nightly Examination of Conscience

Date: _____

Opening Prayer:

My Lord and my God,
I firmly believe that you are here;
that you see me,
that you hear me,
I adore you with profound reverence;
I beg your pardon of my sins,

and the grace to make this time
of prayer fruitful.
My Immaculate Mother,
Saint Joseph my father and lord,
my guardian angel,
intercede for me.

I'm Thankful today for...

Thank God for whatever you are blessed and grateful today.

_____
_____
_____
_____
_____
_____
_____
_____
_____
_____
_____

The Best Version of Myself today

Revisit the times and situations in the past 24 hours of your actions.

_____
_____
_____
_____
_____
_____
_____
_____

My Nightly Examination of Conscience

Date: _____

My Sins & Shortcomings today

Revisit the times and situations in the past 24 hours of your actions.

_____
_____
_____
_____

Ask God for forgiveness for any wrong you have committed
(against Him, yourself and/or another person).

My Resolution for Tomorrow

Ask God to help you to see what He is asking of you and resolve to do it.

_____
_____
_____
_____

My Prayer Requests

Lift up to God anyone and anything you need to pray for today.

_____
_____
_____
_____
_____

Pray the Our Father.

Closing Prayer:

I thank you, My God, for the good resolutions, affections and inspirations that you have communicated to me in this meditation.

I beg your help for putting them into effect. My Immaculate Mother, Saint Joseph my father and lord, my guardian angel, intercede for me.

My Nightly Examination of Conscience

Date: _____

Opening Prayer:

My Lord and my God,
I firmly believe that you are here;
that you see me,
that you hear me,
I adore you with profound reverence;
I beg your pardon of my sins,

and the grace to make this time
of prayer fruitful.
My Immaculate Mother,
Saint Joseph my father and lord,
my guardian angel,
intercede for me.

I'm Thankful today for...

Thank God for whatever you are blessed and grateful today.

_____

_____

_____

_____

_____

_____

_____

_____

_____

_____

_____

The Best Version of Myself today

Revisit the times and situations in the past 24 hours of your actions.

_____

_____

_____

_____

_____

_____

_____

_____

_____

_____

My Nightly Examination of Conscience

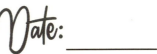

Date: _____

My Sins & Shortcomings today

Revisit the times and situations in the past 24 hours of your actions.

_____

_____

_____

_____

Ask God for forgiveness for any wrong you have committed
(against Him, yourself and/or another person).

My Resolution for Tomorrow

Ask God to help you to see what He is asking of you and resolve to do it.

_____

_____

_____

_____

My Prayer Requests

Lift up to God anyone and anything you need to pray for today.

_____

_____

_____

_____

_____

Pray the Our Father.

Closing Prayer:

I thank you, My God, for the good resolutions, affections and inspirations that you have communicated to me in this meditation.

I beg your help for putting them into effect. My Immaculate Mother, Saint Joseph my father and lord, my guardian angel, intercede for me.

My Nightly Examination of Conscience

Date: _____

Opening Prayer:

My Lord and my God,
I firmly believe that you are here;
that you see me,
that you hear me,
I adore you with profound reverence;
I beg your pardon of my sins,

and the grace to make this time
of prayer fruitful.
My Immaculate Mother,
Saint Joseph my father and lord,
my guardian angel,
intercede for me.

I'm Thankful today for...

Thank God for whatever you are blessed and grateful today.

_____

_____

_____

_____

_____

_____

_____

_____

_____

_____

The Best Version of Myself today

Revisit the times and situations in the past 24 hours of your actions.

_____

_____

_____

_____

_____

_____

_____

_____

_____

My Nightly Examination of Conscience

Date: _____

My Sins & Shortcomings today

Revisit the times and situations in the past 24 hours of your actions.

_____

_____

_____

_____

Ask God for forgiveness for any wrong you have committed
(against Him, yourself and/or another person).

My Resolution for Tomorrow

Ask God to help you to see what He is asking of you and resolve to do it.

_____

_____

_____

_____

My Prayer Requests

Lift up to God anyone and anything you need to pray for today.

_____

_____

_____

_____

_____

Pray the Our Father.

Closing Prayer:

I thank you, My God, for the good resolutions, affections and inspirations that you have communicated to me in this meditation.

I beg your help for putting them into effect. My Immaculate Mother, Saint Joseph my father and lord, my guardian angel, intercede for me.

My Nightly Examination of Conscience

Date: _____

Opening Prayer:

My Lord and my God,
I firmly believe that you are here;
that you see me,
that you hear me,
I adore you with profound reverence;
I beg your pardon of my sins,
and the grace to make this time
of prayer fruitful.
My Immaculate Mother,
Saint Joseph my father and lord,
my guardian angel,
intercede for me.

I'm Thankful today for...

Thank God for whatever you are blessed and grateful today.

_____

_____

_____

_____

_____

_____

_____

_____

_____

_____

_____

The Best Version of Myself today

Revisit the times and situations in the past 24 hours of your actions.

_____

_____

_____

_____

_____

_____

_____

_____

_____

My Nightly Examination of Conscience

Date: _____

My Sins & Shortcomings today

Revisit the times and situations in the past 24 hours of your actions.

_____
_____
_____
_____

Ask God for forgiveness for any wrong you have committed
(against Him, yourself and/or another person).

My Resolution for Tomorrow

Ask God to help you to see what He is asking of you and resolve to do it.

_____
_____
_____

My Prayer Requests

Lift up to God anyone and anything you need to pray for today.

_____
_____
_____
_____
_____

Pray the Our Father.

Closing Prayer:

I thank you, My God, for the good resolutions, affections and inspirations that you have communicated to me in this meditation.

I beg your help for putting them into effect. My Immaculate Mother, Saint Joseph my father and lord, my guardian angel, intercede for me.

My Nightly Examination of Conscience

Date: _____

Opening Prayer:

My Lord and my God,
I firmly believe that you are here;
that you see me,
that you hear me,
I adore you with profound reverence;
I beg your pardon of my sins,
and the grace to make this time
of prayer fruitful.
My Immaculate Mother,
Saint Joseph my father and lord,
my guardian angel,
intercede for me.

I'm Thankful today for...

Thank God for whatever you are blessed and grateful today.

_____
_____
_____
_____
_____
_____
_____
_____
_____
_____
_____

The Best Version of Myself today

Revisit the times and situations in the past 24 hours of your actions.

_____
_____
_____
_____
_____
_____
_____
_____
_____

My Nightly Examination of Conscience

Date: _____

My Sins & Shortcomings today

Revisit the times and situations in the past 24 hours of your actions.

_____
_____
_____
_____

*Ask God for forgiveness for any wrong you have committed
(against Him, yourself and/or another person).*

My Resolution for Tomorrow

Ask God to help you to see what He is asking of you and resolve to do it.

_____
_____
_____
_____

My Prayer Requests

Lift up to God anyone and anything you need to pray for today.

_____
_____
_____
_____
_____

Pray the Our Father.

Closing Prayer:

I thank you, My God, for the good resolutions, affections and inspirations that you have communicated to me in this meditation.

I beg your help for putting them into effect. My Immaculate Mother, Saint Joseph my father and lord, my guardian angel, intercede for me.

My Nightly Examination of Conscience

Date: _____

Opening Prayer:

My Lord and my God,
I firmly believe that you are here;
that you see me,
that you hear me,
I adore you with profound reverence;
I beg your pardon of my sins,

and the grace to make this time
of prayer fruitful.
My Immaculate Mother,
Saint Joseph my father and lord,
my guardian angel,
intercede for me.

I'm Thankful today for...

Thank God for whatever you are blessed and grateful today.

_____
_____
_____
_____
_____
_____
_____
_____
_____
_____
_____

The Best Version of Myself today

Revisit the times and situations in the past 24 hours of your actions.

_____
_____
_____
_____
_____
_____
_____
_____
_____

My
Nightly
Examination
of Conscience

Date: _____

My Sins & Shortcomings today

Revisit the times and situations in the past 24 hours of your actions.

_____

_____

_____

_____

Ask God for forgiveness for any wrong you have committed
(against Him, yourself and/or another person).

My Resolution for Tomorrow

Ask God to help you to see what He is asking of you and resolve to do it.

_____

_____

_____

_____

My Prayer Requests

Lift up to God anyone and anything you need to pray for today.

_____

_____

_____

_____

_____

Pray the Our Father.

Closing Prayer:

I thank you, My God,
for the good resolutions,
affections and inspirations
that you have
communicated to me
in this meditation.

I beg your help for
putting them into effect.
My Immaculate Mother,
Saint Joseph my father and lord,
my guardian angel,
intercede for me.

My Nightly Examination of Conscience

Date: _____

Opening Prayer:

My Lord and my God,
I firmly believe that you are here;
that you see me,
that you hear me,
I adore you with profound reverence;
I beg your pardon of my sins,

and the grace to make this time
of prayer fruitful.
My Immaculate Mother,
Saint Joseph my father and lord,
my guardian angel,
intercede for me.

I'm Thankful today for...

Thank God for whatever you are blessed and grateful today.

_____
_____
_____
_____
_____
_____
_____
_____
_____
_____
_____
_____

The Best Version of Myself today

Revisit the times and situations in the past 24 hours of your actions.

_____
_____
_____
_____
_____
_____
_____
_____
_____
_____

My Nightly Examination of Conscience

Date: _____

My Sins & Shortcomings today

Revisit the times and situations in the past 24 hours of your actions.

_____
_____
_____
_____

*Ask God for forgiveness for any wrong you have committed
(against Him, yourself and/or another person).*

My Resolution for Tomorrow

Ask God to help you to see what He is asking of you and resolve to do it.

_____
_____
_____
_____

My Prayer Requests

Lift up to God anyone and anything you need to pray for today.

_____
_____
_____
_____
_____

Pray the Our Father.

Closing Prayer:

I thank you, My God, for the good resolutions, affections and inspirations that you have communicated to me in this meditation. I beg your help for putting them into effect. My Immaculate Mother, Saint Joseph my father and lord, my guardian angel, intercede for me.

My Nightly Examination of Conscience

Date: _____

Opening Prayer:

My Lord and my God,
I firmly believe that you are here;
that you see me,
that you hear me,
I adore you with profound reverence;
I beg your pardon of my sins,

and the grace to make this time
of prayer fruitful.
My Immaculate Mother,
Saint Joseph my father and lord,
my guardian angel,
intercede for me.

I'm Thankful today for...

Thank God for whatever you are blessed and grateful today.

_____
_____
_____
_____
_____
_____
_____
_____
_____
_____
_____

The Best Version of Myself today

Revisit the times and situations in the past 24 hours of your actions.

_____
_____
_____
_____
_____
_____
_____
_____
_____

Date: _____

My Sins & Shortcomings today

Revisit the times and situations in the past 24 hours of your actions.

_____
_____
_____
_____

*Ask God for forgiveness for any wrong you have committed
(against Him, yourself and/or another person).*

My Resolution for Tomorrow

Ask God to help you to see what He is asking of you and resolve to do it.

_____
_____
_____
_____

My Prayer Requests

Lift up to God anyone and anything you need to pray for today.

_____
_____
_____
_____
_____

Pray the Our Father.

Closing Prayer:

*I thank you, My God,
for the good resolutions,
affections and inspirations
that you have
communicated to me
in this meditation.*

*I beg your help for
putting them into effect.
My Immaculate Mother,
Saint Joseph my father and lord,
my guardian angel,
intercede for me.*

My Nightly Examination of Conscience

Date: _____

Opening Prayer:

My Lord and my God,
I firmly believe that you are here;
that you see me,
that you hear me,
I adore you with profound reverence;
I beg your pardon of my sins,

and the grace to make this time
of prayer fruitful.
My Immaculate Mother,
Saint Joseph my father and lord,
my guardian angel,
intercede for me.

I'm Thankful today for...

Thank God for whatever you are blessed and grateful today.

_____

_____

_____

_____

_____

_____

_____

_____

_____

_____

_____

The Best Version of Myself today

Revisit the times and situations in the past 24 hours of your actions.

_____

_____

_____

_____

_____

_____

_____

_____

_____

_____

My Nightly Examination of Conscience

Date: _____

My Sins & Shortcomings today

Revisit the times and situations in the past 24 hours of your actions.

_____

_____

_____

_____

Ask God for forgiveness for any wrong you have committed
(against Him, yourself and/or another person).

My Resolution for Tomorrow

Ask God to help you to see what He is asking of you and resolve to do it.

_____

_____

_____

_____

My Prayer Requests

Lift up to God anyone and anything you need to pray for today.

_____

_____

_____

_____

_____

Pray the Our Father.

Closing Prayer:

I thank you, My God, for the good resolutions, affections and inspirations that you have communicated to me in this meditation.

I beg your help for putting them into effect. My Immaculate Mother, Saint Joseph my father and lord, my guardian angel, intercede for me.

My Nightly Examination of Conscience

Date: _____

Opening Prayer:

My Lord and my God,
I firmly believe that you are here;
that you see me,
that you hear me,
I adore you with profound reverence;
I beg your pardon of my sins,

and the grace to make this time
of prayer fruitful.
My Immaculate Mother,
Saint Joseph my father and lord,
my guardian angel,
intercede for me.

I'm Thankful today for...

Thank God for whatever you are blessed and grateful today.

_____
_____
_____
_____
_____
_____
_____
_____
_____
_____
_____

The Best Version of Myself today

Revisit the times and situations in the past 24 hours of your actions.

_____
_____
_____
_____
_____
_____
_____
_____
_____

My *Nightly Examination of Conscience*

Date: _____

My Sins & Shortcomings today

Revisit the times and situations in the past 24 hours of your actions.

_____
_____
_____
_____

Ask God for forgiveness for any wrong you have committed
(against Him, yourself and/or another person).

My Resolution for Tomorrow

Ask God to help you to see what He is asking of you and resolve to do it.

_____
_____
_____
_____

My Prayer Requests

Lift up to God anyone and anything you need to pray for today.

_____
_____
_____
_____
_____

Pray the Our Father.

Closing Prayer:

I thank you, My God,
for the good resolutions,
affections and inspirations
that you have
communicated to me
in this meditation.

I beg your help for
putting them into effect.
My Immaculate Mother,
Saint Joseph my father and lord,
my guardian angel,
intercede for me.

My Nightly Examination of Conscience

Date: _____

Opening Prayer:

My Lord and my God,
I firmly believe that you are here;
that you see me,
that you hear me,
I adore you with profound reverence;
I beg your pardon of my sins,

and the grace to make this time
of prayer fruitful.
My Immaculate Mother,
Saint Joseph my father and lord,
my guardian angel,
intercede for me.

I'm Thankful today for...

Thank God for whatever you are blessed and grateful today.

_____

_____

_____

_____

_____

_____

_____

_____

_____

_____

_____

The Best Version of Myself today

Revisit the times and situations in the past 24 hours of your actions.

_____

_____

_____

_____

_____

_____

_____

_____

_____

My Nightly Examination of Conscience

Date: _____

My Sins & Shortcomings today

Revisit the times and situations in the past 24 hours of your actions.

_____
_____
_____
_____

Ask God for forgiveness for any wrong you have committed
(against Him, yourself and/or another person).

My Resolution for Tomorrow

Ask God to help you to see what He is asking of you and resolve to do it.

_____
_____
_____
_____

My Prayer Requests

Lift up to God anyone and anything you need to pray for today.

_____
_____
_____
_____
_____
_____

Pray the Our Father.

Closing Prayer:

I thank you, My God, for the good resolutions, affections and inspirations that you have communicated to me in this meditation.

I beg your help for putting them into effect. My Immaculate Mother, Saint Joseph my father and lord, my guardian angel, intercede for me.

Date: _____

Opening Prayer:

My Lord and my God,
I firmly believe that you are here;
that you see me,
that you hear me,
I adore you with profound reverence;
I beg your pardon of my sins,

and the grace to make this time
of prayer fruitful.
My Immaculate Mother,
Saint Joseph my father and lord,
my guardian angel,
intercede for me.

I'm Thankful today for...

Thank God for whatever you are blessed and grateful today.

_____
_____
_____
_____
_____
_____
_____
_____
_____
_____

The Best Version of Myself today

Revisit the times and situations in the past 24 hours of your actions.

_____
_____
_____
_____
_____
_____
_____
_____
_____

My Nightly Examination of Conscience

Date: _____

My Sins & Shortcomings today

Revisit the times and situations in the past 24 hours of your actions.

_____

_____

_____

_____

Ask God for forgiveness for any wrong you have committed
(against Him, yourself and/or another person).

My Resolution for Tomorrow

Ask God to help you to see what He is asking of you and resolve to do it.

_____

_____

_____

_____

My Prayer Requests

Lift up to God anyone and anything you need to pray for today.

_____

_____

_____

_____

_____

Pray the Our Father.

Closing Prayer:

I thank you, My God, for the good resolutions, affections and inspirations that you have communicated to me in this meditation.

I beg your help for putting them into effect. My Immaculate Mother, Saint Joseph my father and lord, my guardian angel, intercede for me.

My Nightly Examination of Conscience

Date: _____

Opening Prayer:

*My Lord and my God,
I firmly believe that you are here;
that you see me,
that you hear me,
I adore you with profound reverence;
I beg your pardon of my sins,*

*and the grace to make this time
of prayer fruitful.
My Immaculate Mother,
Saint Joseph my father and lord,
my guardian angel,
intercede for me.*

I'm Thankful today for...

Thank God for whatever you are blessed and grateful today.

_____

_____

_____

_____

_____

_____

_____

_____

_____

_____

_____

_____

The Best Version of Myself today

Revisit the times and situations in the past 24 hours of your actions.

_____

_____

_____

_____

_____

_____

_____

_____

_____

_____

_____

My Nightly Examination of Conscience

Date: _____

My Sins & Shortcomings today

Revisit the times and situations in the past 24 hours of your actions.

_____

_____

_____

_____

*Ask God for forgiveness for any wrong you have committed
(against Him, yourself and/or another person).*

My Resolution for Tomorrow

Ask God to help you to see what He is asking of you and resolve to do it.

_____

_____

_____

_____

My Prayer Requests

Lift up to God anyone and anything you need to pray for today.

_____

_____

_____

_____

_____

Pray the Our Father.

Closing Prayer:

I thank you, My God, for the good resolutions, affections and inspirations that you have communicated to me in this meditation.

I beg your help for putting them into effect. My Immaculate Mother, Saint Joseph my father and lord, my guardian angel, intercede for me.

My Nightly Examination of Conscience

Date: _____

Opening Prayer:

My Lord and my God,
I firmly believe that you are here;
that you see me,
that you hear me,
I adore you with profound reverence;
I beg your pardon of my sins,
and the grace to make this time
of prayer fruitful.
My Immaculate Mother,
Saint Joseph my father and lord,
my guardian angel,
intercede for me.

I'm Thankful today for...

Thank God for whatever you are blessed and grateful today.

_____
_____
_____
_____
_____
_____
_____
_____
_____
_____
_____
_____

The Best Version of Myself today

Revisit the times and situations in the past 24 hours of your actions.

_____
_____
_____
_____
_____
_____
_____
_____
_____

My Nightly Examination of Conscience

Date: _____

My Sins & Shortcomings today

Revisit the times and situations in the past 24 hours of your actions.

_____
_____
_____
_____

Ask God for forgiveness for any wrong you have committed
(against Him, yourself and/or another person).

My Resolution for Tomorrow

Ask God to help you to see what He is asking of you and resolve to do it.

_____
_____
_____
_____

My Prayer Requests

Lift up to God anyone and anything you need to pray for today.

_____
_____
_____
_____
_____

Pray the Our Father.

Closing Prayer:

I thank you, My God, for the good resolutions, affections and inspirations that you have communicated to me in this meditation.

I beg your help for putting them into effect. My Immaculate Mother, Saint Joseph my father and lord, my guardian angel, intercede for me.

My Nightly Examination of Conscience

Date: _____

Opening Prayer:

My Lord and my God,
I firmly believe that you are here;
that you see me,
that you hear me,
I adore you with profound reverence;
I beg your pardon of my sins,
and the grace to make this time
of prayer fruitful.
My Immaculate Mother,
Saint Joseph my father and lord,
my guardian angel,
intercede for me.

I'm Thankful today for...

Thank God for whatever you are blessed and grateful today.

_____

_____

_____

_____

_____

_____

_____

_____

_____

_____

_____

The Best Version of Myself today

Revisit the times and situations in the past 24 hours of your actions.

_____

_____

_____

_____

_____

_____

_____

_____

_____

My Nightly Examination of Conscience

Date: _____

My Sins & Shortcomings today

Revisit the times and situations in the past 24 hours of your actions.

_____
_____
_____
_____

Ask God for forgiveness for any wrong you have committed
(against Him, yourself and/or another person).

My Resolution for Tomorrow

Ask God to help you to see what He is asking of you and resolve to do it.

_____
_____
_____
_____

My Prayer Requests

Lift up to God anyone and anything you need to pray for today.

_____
_____
_____
_____

Pray the Our Father.

Closing Prayer:

I thank you, My God, for the good resolutions, affections and inspirations that you have communicated to me in this meditation.

I beg your help for putting them into effect. My Immaculate Mother, Saint Joseph my father and lord, my guardian angel, intercede for me.

My Nightly Examination of Conscience

Date: _____

Opening Prayer:

My Lord and my God,
I firmly believe that you are here;
that you see me,
that you hear me,
I adore you with profound reverence;
I beg your pardon of my sins,

and the grace to make this time
of prayer fruitful.
My Immaculate Mother,
Saint Joseph my father and lord,
my guardian angel,
intercede for me.

I'm Thankful today for...

Thank God for whatever you are blessed and grateful today.

_____
_____
_____
_____
_____
_____
_____
_____
_____
_____
_____

The Best Version of Myself today

Revisit the times and situations in the past 24 hours of your actions.

_____
_____
_____
_____
_____
_____
_____
_____
_____
_____

My Nightly Examination of Conscience

Date: _____

My Sins & Shortcomings today

Revisit the times and situations in the past 24 hours of your actions.

_____

_____

_____

_____

Ask God for forgiveness for any wrong you have committed
(against Him, yourself and/or another person).

My Resolution for Tomorrow

Ask God to help you to see what He is asking of you and resolve to do it.

_____

_____

_____

_____

My Prayer Requests

Lift up to God anyone and anything you need to pray for today.

_____

_____

_____

_____

_____

Pray the Our Father.

Closing Prayer:

I thank you, My God, for the good resolutions, affections and inspirations that you have communicated to me in this meditation.

I beg your help for putting them into effect. My Immaculate Mother, Saint Joseph my father and lord, my guardian angel, intercede for me.

My Nightly Examination of Conscience

Date: _____

Opening Prayer:

My Lord and my God,
I firmly believe that you are here;
that you see me,
that you hear me,
I adore you with profound reverence;
I beg your pardon of my sins,

and the grace to make this time
of prayer fruitful.
My Immaculate Mother,
Saint Joseph my father and lord,
my guardian angel,
intercede for me.

I'm Thankful today for...

Thank God for whatever you are blessed and grateful today.

_____
_____
_____
_____
_____
_____
_____
_____
_____
_____
_____
_____

The Best Version of Myself today

Revisit the times and situations in the past 24 hours of your actions.

_____
_____
_____
_____
_____
_____
_____
_____
_____
_____

 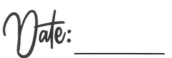

My Sins & Shortcomings today

Revisit the times and situations in the past 24 hours of your actions.

_____

_____

_____

_____

Ask God for forgiveness for any wrong you have committed
(against Him, yourself and/or another person).

My Resolution for Tomorrow

Ask God to help you to see what He is asking of you and resolve to do it.

_____

_____

_____

_____

My Prayer Requests

Lift up to God anyone and anything you need to pray for today.

_____

_____

_____

_____

_____

Pray the Our Father.

Closing Prayer:

I thank you, My God,
for the good resolutions,
affections and inspirations
that you have
communicated to me
in this meditation.

I beg your help for
putting them into effect.
My Immaculate Mother,
Saint Joseph my father and lord,
my guardian angel,
intercede for me.

My Nightly Examination of Conscience

Date: _____

Opening Prayer:

My Lord and my God,
I firmly believe that you are here;
that you see me,
that you hear me,
I adore you with profound reverence;
I beg your pardon of my sins,

and the grace to make this time
of prayer fruitful.
My Immaculate Mother,
Saint Joseph my father and lord,
my guardian angel,
intercede for me.

I'm Thankful today for...

Thank God for whatever you are blessed and grateful today.

_____
_____
_____
_____
_____
_____
_____
_____
_____
_____
_____
_____

The Best Version of Myself today

Revisit the times and situations in the past 24 hours of your actions.

_____
_____
_____
_____
_____
_____
_____
_____
_____
_____

My Nightly Examination of Conscience

Date: _____

My Sins & Shortcomings today

Revisit the times and situations in the past 24 hours of your actions.

_____

_____

_____

_____

Ask God for forgiveness for any wrong you have committed
(against Him, yourself and/or another person).

My Resolution for Tomorrow

Ask God to help you to see what He is asking of you and resolve to do it.

_____

_____

_____

_____

My Prayer Requests

Lift up to God anyone and anything you need to pray for today.

_____

_____

_____

_____

_____

Pray the Our Father.

Closing Prayer:

I thank you, My God, for the good resolutions, affections and inspirations that you have communicated to me in this meditation.

I beg your help for putting them into effect. My Immaculate Mother, Saint Joseph my father and lord, my guardian angel, intercede for me.

Date: _____

Opening Prayer:

My Lord and my God,
I firmly believe that you are here;
that you see me,
that you hear me,
I adore you with profound reverence;
I beg your pardon of my sins,

and the grace to make this time
of prayer fruitful.
My Immaculate Mother,
Saint Joseph my father and lord,
my guardian angel,
intercede for me.

I'm Thankful today for...

Thank God for whatever you are blessed and grateful today.

_____
_____
_____
_____
_____
_____
_____
_____
_____
_____
_____

The Best Version of Myself today

Revisit the times and situations in the past 24 hours of your actions.

_____
_____
_____
_____
_____
_____
_____
_____
_____

My Nightly Examination of Conscience

Date: _____

My Sins & Shortcomings today

Revisit the times and situations in the past 24 hours of your actions.

_____

_____

_____

_____

*Ask God for forgiveness for any wrong you have committed
(against Him, yourself and/or another person).*

My Resolution for Tomorrow

Ask God to help you to see what He is asking of you and resolve to do it.

_____

_____

_____

_____

My Prayer Requests

Lift up to God anyone and anything you need to pray for today.

_____

_____

_____

_____

_____

Pray the Our Father.

Closing Prayer:

*I thank you, My God,
for the good resolutions,
affections and inspirations
that you have
communicated to me
In this meditation.*

*I beg your help for
putting them into effect.
My Immaculate Mother,
Saint Joseph my father and lord,
my guardian angel,
intercede for me.*

My Nightly Examination of Conscience

Date: _____

Opening Prayer:

My Lord and my God,
I firmly believe that you are here;
that you see me,
that you hear me,
I adore you with profound reverence;
I beg your pardon of my sins,
and the grace to make this time
of prayer fruitful.
My Immaculate Mother,
Saint Joseph my father and lord,
my guardian angel,
intercede for me.

I'm Thankful today for...

Thank God for whatever you are blessed and grateful today.

_____
_____
_____
_____
_____
_____
_____
_____
_____
_____
_____

The Best Version of Myself today

Revisit the times and situations in the past 24 hours of your actions.

_____
_____
_____
_____
_____
_____
_____
_____
_____

My Nightly Examination of Conscience

Date: _____

My Sins & Shortcomings today

Revisit the times and situations in the past 24 hours of your actions.

_____
_____
_____
_____

Ask God for forgiveness for any wrong you have committed
(against Him, yourself and/or another person).

My Resolution for Tomorrow

Ask God to help you to see what He is asking of you and resolve to do it.

_____
_____
_____
_____

My Prayer Requests

Lift up to God anyone and anything you need to pray for today.

_____
_____
_____
_____
_____

Pray the Our Father.

Closing Prayer:

I thank you, My God, for the good resolutions, affections and inspirations that you have communicated to me in this meditation.

I beg your help for putting them into effect. My Immaculate Mother, Saint Joseph my father and lord, my guardian angel, intercede for me.

My Nightly Examination of Conscience

Date: _____

Opening Prayer:

My Lord and my God,
I firmly believe that you are here;
that you see me,
that you hear me,
I adore you with profound reverence;
I beg your pardon of my sins,

and the grace to make this time
of prayer fruitful.
My Immaculate Mother,
Saint Joseph my father and lord,
my guardian angel,
intercede for me.

I'm Thankful today for...

Thank God for whatever you are blessed and grateful today.

_____
_____
_____
_____
_____
_____
_____
_____
_____
_____
_____

The Best Version of Myself today

Revisit the times and situations in the past 24 hours of your actions.

_____
_____
_____
_____
_____
_____
_____
_____
_____
_____

My Nightly Examination of Conscience

Date: _____

My Sins & Shortcomings today

Revisit the times and situations in the past 24 hours of your actions.

_____

_____

_____

_____

*Ask God for forgiveness for any wrong you have committed
(against Him, yourself and/or another person).*

My Resolution for Tomorrow

Ask God to help you to see what He is asking of you and resolve to do it.

_____

_____

_____

_____

My Prayer Requests

Lift up to God anyone and anything you need to pray for today.

_____

_____

_____

_____

_____

Pray the Our Father.

Closing Prayer:

I thank you, My God, for the good resolutions, affections and inspirations that you have communicated to me in this meditation. I beg your help for putting them into effect. My Immaculate Mother, Saint Joseph my father and lord, my guardian angel, intercede for me.

Date: _____

Opening Prayer:

My Lord and my God,
I firmly believe that you are here;
that you see me,
that you hear me,
I adore you with profound reverence;
I beg your pardon of my sins,
and the grace to make this time
of prayer fruitful.
My Immaculate Mother,
Saint Joseph my father and lord,
my guardian angel,
intercede for me.

I'm Thankful today for...

Thank God for whatever you are blessed and grateful today.

_____

_____

_____

_____

_____

_____

_____

_____

_____

_____

The Best Version of Myself today

Revisit the times and situations in the past 24 hours of your actions.

_____

_____

_____

_____

_____

_____

_____

_____

_____

My Nightly Examination of Conscience

Date: _____

My Sins & Shortcomings today

Revisit the times and situations in the past 24 hours of your actions.

_____
_____
_____
_____

Ask God for forgiveness for any wrong you have committed
(against Him, yourself and/or another person).

My Resolution for Tomorrow

Ask God to help you to see what He is asking of you and resolve to do it.

_____
_____
_____
_____

My Prayer Requests

Lift up to God anyone and anything you need to pray for today.

_____
_____
_____
_____
_____

Pray the Our Father.

Closing Prayer:

I thank you, My God, for the good resolutions, affections and inspirations that you have communicated to me In this meditation.

I beg your help for putting them into effect. My Immaculate Mother, Saint Joseph my father and lord, my guardian angel, intercede for me.

My Nightly Examination of Conscience

Date: _____

Opening Prayer:

My Lord and my God,
I firmly believe that you are here;
that you see me,
that you hear me,
I adore you with profound reverence;
I beg your pardon of my sins,
and the grace to make this time
of prayer fruitful.
My Immaculate Mother,
Saint Joseph my father and lord,
my guardian angel,
intercede for me.

I'm Thankful today for...

Thank God for whatever you are blessed and grateful today.

_____
_____
_____
_____
_____
_____
_____
_____
_____
_____
_____

The Best Version of Myself today

Revisit the times and situations in the past 24 hours of your actions.

_____
_____
_____
_____
_____
_____
_____
_____

My Nightly Examination of Conscience

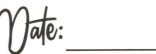

Date: _____

My Sins & Shortcomings today

Revisit the times and situations in the past 24 hours of your actions.

_____

_____

_____

_____

Ask God for forgiveness for any wrong you have committed
(against Him, yourself and/or another person).

My Resolution for Tomorrow

Ask God to help you to see what He is asking of you and resolve to do it.

_____

_____

_____

_____

My Prayer Requests

Lift up to God anyone and anything you need to pray for today.

_____

_____

_____

_____

_____

Pray the Our Father.

Closing Prayer:

I thank you, My God, for the good resolutions, affections and inspirations that you have communicated to me in this meditation.

I beg your help for putting them into effect. My Immaculate Mother, Saint Joseph my father and lord, my guardian angel, intercede for me.

My Nightly Examination of Conscience

Date: _____

Opening Prayer:

My Lord and my God,
I firmly believe that you are here;
that you see me,
that you hear me,
I adore you with profound reverence;
I beg your pardon of my sins,

and the grace to make this time
of prayer fruitful.
My Immaculate Mother,
Saint Joseph my father and lord,
my guardian angel,
intercede for me.

I'm Thankful today for...

Thank God for whatever you are blessed and grateful today.

_____
_____
_____
_____
_____
_____
_____
_____
_____
_____
_____
_____

The Best Version of Myself today

Revisit the times and situations in the past 24 hours of your actions.

_____
_____
_____
_____
_____
_____
_____
_____
_____

My Nightly Examination of Conscience

Date: _____

My Sins & Shortcomings today

Revisit the times and situations in the past 24 hours of your actions.

_____
_____
_____
_____

Ask God for forgiveness for any wrong you have committed
(against Him, yourself and/or another person).

My Resolution for Tomorrow

Ask God to help you to see what He is asking of you and resolve to do it.

_____
_____
_____
_____

My Prayer Requests

Lift up to God anyone and anything you need to pray for today.

_____
_____
_____
_____
_____

Pray the Our Father.

Closing Prayer:

I thank you, My God, for the good resolutions, affections and inspirations that you have communicated to me in this meditation. I beg your help for putting them into effect. My Immaculate Mother, Saint Joseph my father and lord, my guardian angel, intercede for me.

To re-order your
My Nightly Examination of Conscience
Visit
Amazon.com/author/domchu
Thank you!

"To reform. Every day a little.
This has to be your constant task
if you really want to become a saint."
(St. Josemaría Escrivá)

Other Titles by Dom Chu at
Amazon.com/author/domchu

All Saints Inspiration Notebook
ASIN: B0BKS3JTPB (Paperback)
ASIN: B0BKXMRQN8 (Hardcover)

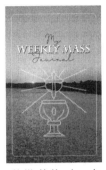

My Weekly Mass Journal
ASIN: B09CKJR24M

Lectio Divina for Starters
ASIN: B09JJ98ND9

Cute Catholic Kawaii Saints Coloring Book
ASIN: B09DDV4VR1

Offer It Up To Jesus
ASIN: B0BJ33FX2V (Paperback)
ASIN: B0BJ7XBG8M (Ebook)

Color & Pray The Holy Rosary
ASIN: B09XZHLXL5

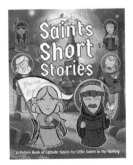

Saints Short Stories
ASIN: B09FNY2WG1 (Paperback)
ASIN: B09FKPV4ML (Ebook)

Superhero Saints Short Stories
ASIN: B0CH2NN4VX (Paperback)
ASIN: B0CHGLQSVH (Ebook)

Scissor Skills: Saints with Superpowers
ASIN: B0CJ3VVWL6

Please share your thoughts &
Help others make a great choice.
Visit
Amazon.com/author/domchu
And post a quick review of this journal.
Thank you!

Find
Socials, Merch & Channel Online!
FOLLOW, LIKE & SHOP

Amazon.com/author/domchu

Etsy.com/shop/artjuniverse

Artjuniverse.redbubble.com

Teepublic.com/user/artjuniverse

Youtube.com/@SanctiSagas

Made in the USA
Columbia, SC
08 May 2025

57710088R00064